THE WORLD AROUND US

ON THE PLAYGROUND

Our First Talk About Prejudice

Dr. Jillian Roberts   Illustrations by Jane Heinrichs

ORCA BOOK PUBLISHERS

I dedicate this book to the Sisters of St. Ann, whose kindness, love, compassion and social activism inspire me daily. Thank you for giving me a spiritual home.
—JR

To my teachers in the Hanover School Division. Thank you for all the guidance and inspiration.
—JH

Library and Archives Canada Cataloguing in Publication

Roberts, Jillian, 1971–, author
On the playground: our first talk about prejudice / Dr. Jillian Roberts;
illustrations by Jane Heinrichs.
(The world around us)

Issued in print and electronic formats.
ISBN 978-1-4598-2091-3 (hardcover).—ISBN 978-1-4598-2092-0 (pdf).—
ISBN 978-1-4598-2093-7 (epub)

1. Prejudices—Juvenile literature. I. Heinrichs, Jane, 1982–, illustrator
II. Title.
HM1091.R63 2019   j303.3'85   c2018-904786-0
c2018-904787-9

Summary: Using illustrations, full-color photographs and straightforward text, this
nonfiction picture book introduces the topic of prejudice to young readers.

Simultaneously published in Canada and the United States in 2018
Library of Congress Control Number: 2018954151

MIX
Paper from
responsible sources
FSC® C016245
FSC
www.fsc.org

*Orca Book Publishers is dedicated to preserving the environment and has
printed this book on Forest Stewardship Council® certified paper.*

Orca Book Publishers gratefully acknowledges the support for its
publishing programs provided by the following agencies: the Government of Canada,
the Canada Council for the Arts and the Province of British Columbia
through the BC Arts Council and the Book Publishing Tax Credit.

Cover and interior art by Jane Heinrichs
Artwork created using English watercolors and
Japanese brush pens on Italian watercolor paper.
Edited by Liz Kemp
Design by Rachel Page

Front cover photos (left to right):
Stocksy.com, iStock.com, Stocksy.com
Back cover photos: Shutterstock.com (left) and iStock.com
Interior photos:
Shutterstock.com: © Ovu0ng p. 5, SpeedKingz p. 6, Tom Wang p. 7,
Monkey Business Images p. 8, Casezy idea p. 15, DGLimages p. 22
iStock.com: © tomazl p. 9, djedzura p. 10, Wavebreakmedia p. 13,
SolStock p. 16, FatCamera p. 17, fstop123 p. 20, FatCamera p. 21,
FatCamera p. 23, monkeybusinessimages p. 24, Lisa5201 p. 28
Stocksy.com: © Dina Giangregorio p. 11, Kerry Murphy p. 14,
Anya Brewley Schultheiss p. 19, Kristen Curette Hines p. 27
Unsplash.com: Cel Lisboa p. 18

ORCA BOOK PUBLISHERS
orcabook.com

Printed and bound in Canada.

22 21 20 19 • 4 3 2 1

○–○

When you are with other children at school

or on the playground, you may hear unkind things being
said to or about other people. Sometimes people are
teased or made fun of because they're different.

Seeing this behavior or hearing these words might make you feel
angry, sad or confused. It's good to question what you hear other people
say and how other people act, especially when it feels hurtful.

○–○–○–○–○–○–○–   —○–○–○–○–○–○–○

When I was on the playground today,
I saw a boy getting teased and bullied.
The other kids were calling him names.
I felt bad for him.

I understand how you feel. I feel the same way when I see mean things happening around me. The world can be a complicated and confusing place. It's hard to know what to do in these situations, even as an adult.

What is it called when something like this happens?

We call this kind of behavior *harassment*. And when someone is harassed because they are different, it's often due to a *prejudice* held by the person who is being mean.

What Is Harassment?

Harassment is when a person says something hurtful to someone else, or threatens or intimidates them. It includes a person touching another in a way they do not want or that makes them uncomfortable.

What Is Prejudice?

Prejudice is when someone decides what another person is like before getting to know them. Their opinion is based on that person's different race, religion, sex, age or ability.

Why would someone pick on a person just for being different?

Picking on someone because they are different—which is acting in a way that is *prejudiced*—is something people learn. Children who say unkind things probably heard important adults in their lives saying similar things. And those adults may believe that being different is bad.

Why do adults
say mean things?

Adults aren't perfect. Just like children, they make mistakes and can be mean sometimes. And beliefs about other people's differences are often passed along from generation to generation—you may have the same thoughts and feelings as your parents do, who may have the same thoughts and feelings as *their* parents, your grandparents. These mean or disrespectful ideas can be passed down from one generation to the next without anyone realizing it or thinking about whether these thoughts and feelings are right or wrong.

Sometimes people hurt others because they are afraid of what they don't know or don't understand. And sometimes they do it because they were once hurt like that themselves.

How did that boy feel when those kids were so mean to him?

People who are bullied feel a lot of different emotions—anger, sadness and fear. They could feel lonely, misunderstood and excluded. It could be hard for them to get over those bad feelings, especially if mean things happen to them a lot.

Types of Prejudice Include:

Racism: Believing that one race, or a group of people with similar characteristics, is better than another.

Sexism: Believing that one gender is better than another.

Homophobia: Feeling negativity or aversion toward people who are homosexual.

Ageism: Discriminating against people of a particular age group, especially the elderly.

Ableism: Discriminating against people who have disabilities.

I felt angry too when I saw what was happening. I think it's wrong.

Yes, harassment and prejudice *are* wrong. It's natural to feel angry when you see people being hurtful to others.

Even though there are differences between us, we are all equally important. Each one of us deserves love, respect and equal opportunity, regardless of what we look like, how we sound or how we live our lives. Learning to understand and appreciate what makes us diverse, and to see past differences that may be scary or misunderstood, helps us accept one another as we are.

What can I do to help? What could I have done for that boy on the playground?

If you see something happening on the playground, in your classroom or somewhere else, you can go get a parent, teacher or adult you trust and ask for help. You can approach the child who has been hurt and check in on them. Introducing yourself, if you don't know them, or just saying hi might make both of you feel better.

Take some time to look at yourself. Think about whether you have any thoughts or ideas that could be prejudiced or hurtful to others.

It can be really difficult to look at ourselves like that whether we are children or adults, but it's the first step in changing for the better.

Sometimes people are really mixed up. They do not understand the difference between right and wrong. But let's be clear: It is always wrong to intentionally hurt someone. And it is always right to try and help those who are hurt.

Meet Sophie Kamlish

Sophie is a Paralympic athlete from Bath, UK. She inspired one of the characters drawn for this book. When Sophie was nine, she had her lower leg amputated due to a birth defect. Now she runs using a prosthetic blade (a device that attaches to her body like an artificial limb and is used for running). Sophie is a world champion in the 100-meter sprint.

Sophie once wrote that her school days were not the happiest of her life: "It was never one big horrible thing that I experienced. It was the tiny things that added up and those are the sort of things that people don't see as offensive when they say them. I think it's thoughtlessness rather than nastiness. But you internalize those things and you can end up with the idea that disability is something negative, and that is the main thing that needs to change. Disability isn't something that is bad or needs to be cured. It's just another cool part of the world and I hope that change is happening in schools."

The key to respect and acceptance is understanding. Take time to learn about the many diverse people in the world around us. Look for things we share in common, as well as differences you can admire or appreciate. There are so many!

Then share what you're learning with the other kids and adults in your life. That's right—you can set a good example for grown-ups!

Think carefully when you hear another person say something that sounds like it might be hurtful or based on prejudice.

You don't have to believe something just because somebody told you it's true, especially if it feels wrong. Use your own learning and knowledge about the world around you to make up your mind. Or ask a grown-up you trust what they think.

We can practice being good role models for the people around us. We can work against prejudice by behaving in ways that are *inclusive* and *respectful* of everyone.

Ask your friends about their families, their beliefs, their cultures and traditions. If someone has differences you are curious about, ask about them. Understand, though, that sometimes it's hard to talk about differences, so be respectful if someone doesn't want to share.

What Is Inclusivity?

Inclusivity is the practice of acting in ways that include everyone and promote a sense of belonging for all people. An example of inclusivity is when schools have ramps that make it easier for people who use wheelchairs or motorized devices to get in and out of the building.

What Is Respect?

Respect is when you think about the feelings, wishes, rights or traditions of others—and of yourself. To respect other people means that you accept their differences and understand that other people are as important as you are. To respect yourself means you believe in your own worth and in standing up for yourself. It allows you to recognize when others aren't being kind to you or are acting in a way that makes you uncomfortable.

Learning about others, changing for the better and standing up to prejudice help make the world a safer and more respectful, inclusive place for everyone.

A Note from Dr. Jillian Roberts, Author and Child Psychologist

When I was growing up, it was common to see other kids being bullied on the playground because they were different. Perhaps they looked different or unique in some way, or perhaps they were born in a different country. Whatever the reason, these kids were taunted and teased. Much to my shame, I remember doing nothing. As I grew up, I came to understand that this was not the right choice. A better choice would have been to reach out to these other kids and offer them my friendship. I could have asked them to sit beside me at lunch. I could have invited them to play with my group. And, with the kids who were from different countries, I could have tried to learn more about their cultures and traditions. Instead of just watching the bullying happening around me, I could have been a child who made a difference. I encourage all readers of this book to make better choices than I did. You have the power to make your corner of the world a better place!

Resources

Print

Baldacchino, Christine. *Morris Micklewhite and the Tangerine Dress*. Toronto: Groundwood Books, 2014.

Choi, Yangsook. *The Name Jar*. Toronto: Dragonfly Books, 2003.

de la Peña, Matt. *Last Stop on Market Street*. New York: G.P. Putnam's Sons Books for Young Readers, 2015.

Roberts, Dr. Jillian. *What Makes Us Unique? Our First Talk about Diversity*. Victoria, BC: Orca Book Publishers, 2016.

Spilsbury, Louise. *Children in Our World: Racism and Intolerance*. New York: Barron's Educational Series, 2018.

Online

FamilySparks—Resources for parents, teachers and others who support children: familysparks.com

One Globe Kids–All Friends—App for kids from Common Sense Media, an organization dedicated to improving the lives of parents, teachers and advocates: commonsensemedia.org/app-reviews/one-globe-kids-friends-around-the-world

Pink Shirt Day—Campaign that raises awareness of bullying and funds to support anti-bullying programs: pinkshirtday.ca

PREVNet (Promoting Relationships and Eliminating Violence Network)—Research and resources for kids, teens, parents and educators: prevnet.ca

Sophie Kamlish—Read more about the Paralympic athlete on her blog: sophiekamlish.wixsite.com/website

StopBullying.gov—Resources and information for kids, parents and teachers: stopbullying.gov

Teaching Tolerance—Classroom ideas and lesson plans for educators: tolerance.org

The Wonderment—A site where kids can connect and collaborate with kids around the globe: thewonderment.com

THE WORLD AROUND US series

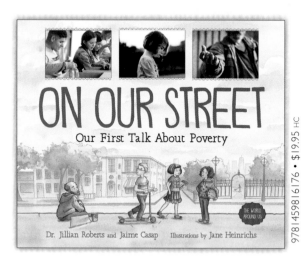

ON OUR STREET
Our First Talk About Poverty

Dr. Jillian Roberts and Jaime Casap   Illustrations by Jane Heinrichs

9781459816176 • $19.95 HC

ON THE NEWS
Our First Talk About Tragedy

Dr. Jillian Roberts   Illustrations by Jane Heinrichs

9781459817845 • $19.95 HC

ON THE INTERNET
Our First Talk About Online Safety

Dr. Jillian Roberts   Illustrations by Jane Heinrichs

9781459820944 • $19.95 HC

Child psychologist Dr. Jillian Roberts covers topics such as:

- poverty and homelessness
- tragedy and disaster
- prejudice and bullying
- Internet safety
- body health and consent
- environmental stewardship

These inquiry-based books are an excellent cross-curricular resource encouraging children to explore and discuss important issues and **foster their own compassion and empathy**.

AGES 6–8 • 32 PAGES
FULL-COLOR PHOTOGRAPHS • RESOURCES INCLUDED

www.TheWorldAroundUsSeries.com